DUSTY DAYS

DUSTY DAYS

POEMS

by

John Urban

Dusty Days
Copyright © 2018 by John Urban

Book design by River Sanctuary Graphic Arts

ISBN 978-1-935914-86-0

Printed in the United States of America

In a Foyer appeared in *Jet Fuel Review* Issue 11 2016
Lewis University, Illinois and *Aphorisms For a New Science* in
Sound & Literary Art Book Issue 13, Slippery Rock University, PA

Contact author at:
johnurb@sbcglobal.net

Additional copies available from:
www.riversanctuarypublishing.com
amazon.com

RIVER SANCTUARY PUBLISHING
P.O. Box 1561
Felton, California 95018
www.riversanctuarypublishing.com
Dedicated to the awakening of the New Earth

Contents

Preludes

I

The highest music speaks.

II

Words, worlds.

III

True music heals.

Nature

Flesh of land, bone of rock;
Shaggy, lion-headed Palms.

*

Autumn, a dark Spring.

*

Upon a glassy creek
The pale, scattered leaves speak.

*

The Pacific, light; the Atlantic, dark.

Emily

Heavenly Emily.

*

Poems are Ponds.

*

The metaphors are minnows.

Personages

A gnome's rugged home,
Rock beneath root of tree.

*

Edwin Markham, the Walt
Whitman of San Jose.

*

A metal-yellow sky, *Atlas Shrugged*.

*

L. Frank Baum's *The Land of Oz*,
The fragrant rose of a Fairy Tale.

Four Thoughts On Thinking

To think is to plow.

*

Logic is necessary for Reason,
But not sufficient.

*

Reason is creative, but few think.

*

Reason runs everywhere.

Twilight, a window between the worlds.

CALIFORNIA QUARTET

I

To the Sierra Madre

Sandy creams, sage greens;
Chalky red and chalky yellow trucks.

In the distance, the bare rock backs
Of the mountains—the dry, wrinkled hills.

At road's edge, cloudy, lace-like broom,
And parti-colored leaves of poison oak.

I lifted my eyes to the silent, beckoning blue.

In the distance, the bare rock backs
Of the mountains—the dry, wrinkled hills.

II

Dusty Days

———————

Dusty days
In San Jose

Leaves of light
Dryly bright.

Gathering juices,
Sweet and deep

Upon the ridges
Bluish fogs sleep.

III

Aphrodite, California

Golden Aphrodite of the beautiful body,
Foam-born goddess, mistress of congregated oak,
Of shining tassels of Spanish oats—the sovereign
Of your skies, the ardent, amber pendent of the Sun.

IV

Turquoise
Sunset
With Palms

———————

Blank blue
California pool.

Tawny slope
Sprinkled Oak.

Egyptian,
To an Octave

Tum's golden foot
Gilds the Western Steppes.

Our birth here
Was a kind of death,
A settling of ourselves,
As it were, into soil.

Camels amble desert-wise;
Sacred stones, sunlit tombs.

Nothing as Something

Why is there being at all and not rather nothing?

Heidegger

Because Being is a concomitant of Nothingness
And Nothingness a concomitant of Being; that is,
Being could not be Being without a substratum
Of Nothing against which, as it were, to assert itself,
And Nothing could not be Nothing without Being being
Subtracted from Being to leave Nothing as a residuum.

After Aristotle

Within the face of woman lies a man's body;
Within the face of a man lies a woman's.

When a man and a woman commingle,
These other two bodies also mingle.

Thus, in the union of a man and a woman
There exist not two, but four parties,
And the involvement is correspondingly mixed.

APHORISMS FOR A NEW SCIENCE

APHORISMS FOR A NEW SCIENCE

I

We move through Space; Time moves through us.

II

Science, devoted thought; Art, thoughtful devotion.

III

Art, the projection of ideas into matter;
Science, the perception of ideas (laws) in matter.

IV

Perception, to an attentive consciousness,
Suggests essence; consciousness, through the mind,
Thereby moves into things.

V

Cryptic Physics—arthritic, electric arcs.

VI

In a corrupt age, even Mathematics is corrupt.

VII

An Idea creates order; thus, a Cosmos.

VIII

The universe is cradled in the arms of the Duad.

IX

Infinity, the womb out of which all things are born.

A
One Word
Poem

Aridzona.

Little Aphorisms

———————————

1.

Time and Space, the parents; motion, the child.

2.

To measure Space takes Time;
To measure Time takes Space.

3.

What Space creates, Time destroys.

4.

Concepts, the matter of mind.

5.

Time is the essence of Science; of Art, Eternity.

The Garden of Truth

A perception, planted in the soil of consciousness
And watered attentively, brings forth the blossom of a concept,
Which two together bear the fruit of Truth.

TWO ACADEMIC POEMS

In a Foyer

A golden-framed oil glistens,
Darkly marked *New York 1927.*

Outside, in the schoolyard below,
Boys knuckle down in the dirt.

Bookman

Words from and for John Ashbery

Tangled versions of the truth,
Stories worn from telling;
You conjure them into existence,
Only to say they are here.

The slow and declining day
Opens new avenues into the town
Along which the light travels,
A certain richness of particulars.

After Words

A resistant heart blocks thought.

*

In the end, all Art is Religious Art.

*

To think the good life is Philosophy;
To live it, Religion.

*

We lift the hands of our hearts to the above.

www.ingramcontent.com/pod-product-compliance
Lightning Source LLC
Chambersburg PA
CBHW021919040426
42448CB00007B/817